DIVINE FOUNDATION

Michelle Bond

authorHOUSE®

AuthorHouse™
1663 Liberty Drive
Bloomington, IN 47403
www.authorhouse.com
Phone: 1 (800) 839-8640

Published by AuthorHouse   09/24/2016

ISBN: 978-1-5246-1378-5 (sc)
ISBN: 978-1-5246-1377-8 (e)

Print information available on the last page.

Any people depicted in stock imagery provided by Thinkstock are models, and such images are being used for illustrative purposes only.
Certain stock imagery © Thinkstock.

This book is printed on acid-free paper.

Scripture quotations marked KJV are from the Holy Bible, King James Version (Authorized Version), first published in 1611. Quoted from the KJV Classic Reference Bible, Copyright ©1983 by the Zondervan Corporation.

Recovering from a broken spirit takes an inner strength that you get from people you love, a setting that is filled with a positive influence.

Once we accept help and our fragile spirit then all will get better with time. Our spirit is resilient and can weather so much. It is the challenges that make us stronger for ourselves and others. If we keep that in mind we are all better for it. The world will be a better place and we will be better people.

By Lorraine D Lira

My leadership is under the direction of the Lord!
Psalm 32:8
I will instruct thee and teach thee in the way which thou shalt go
I will guide thee with mine eyes

I was able to take a counter to over a half a million dollars, growing the counter by adding a part-timer to the mix. The part-timer I hired happened to be a customer whom I had put on the product. Let's talk a little about how I was able to grow the counter. It goes back to *treating people the way you want to be treated and* being able to listen to your customers with your heart rather than looking at their pocketbooks. That will bring satisfaction to you and your customer. I would say to my customers, "Give me a year, and I will show you a lifetime of beauty!"

As I listened with my heart and wrote down the customer's concerns, we planned together a product line to make her or him feel beautiful. We went from preparing the skin to a massage to massaging hands and feet, to the spa room at that retail store that was always full. After I gave a massage, it was time for a makeup lesson. I believe that if you teach customers how to use product and makeup, they will get a full understanding of how to take care of their skin. You have then created a loyal relationship with your customer. When your customer comes back to see you, you have all information on file and can update the file. You would never go to a doctor's office without having a file, would you? I hope not!

Within two years, I was able to move up to the position of account coordinator. At this point, great leadership and great partnership played a big part in expanding our region from 3.6 to 4.2 percent. I have been an account coordinator for fourteen years, and during those years I was also hired to become a trainer. I had to turn down the position because I was unable to move at the time.

Working with my beauty advisors gives me such pleasure. When I first started out, I had sixteen stores and fifty beauty advisors. I have to say that I was always number one in making sure my beauty advisors were certified in massage and makeup. How did I do it? By partnering up with my beauty advisors. Then I paired them in teams to help one another. I also had them form a sisterhood with my other stores, which made them unstoppable. If we needed to borrow anything for events from another store, we were able to help one another.

Our events weren't just water and cookies. Partnering up with the beauty advisor six months in advance to plan events is key. We look at the highest days in the week and weekend within the last six months to plan a key theme event. This excites the team, and everybody takes part in it. I have had some very successful events that a team ran on a weekday, focusing on a product of the day and partnering up with other departments to help promote the event; it resulted in sales 3 percent above our event goal. An event can be anything from a workshop to train the customers on makeup to a product promotion or massage to taking a glamour shot. You want to lay down the red carpet to make the customer feel like the queen of England!

My objective is to always stay focused on delivering volume growth, improving beauty advisor behavior through training and coaching, and partnering up with the beauty advisor to help her understand that this is her business and I am here to help in any way I can. Account coordinators have to wear many hats and have many jobs, including managing, training, event planning and execution, hiring, and communicating effectively. I would not trade this job for the world. If you can wake up with a smile on your face because you enjoy what you do, then you have found your calling. I feel good that I can do that.

Training the beauty advisors also includes their business goals. As their leader, I want to work closely with them to help them achieve them. We start by writing down their goals, and then we begin to plan. Great events and great retail numbers give great results, resulting in promotion to bigger counters with more responsibility.

Preparing for the Big Bonus

Twice a year, we prepare for the big bonus with a meeting that includes a counter manager, the executive trainer, and me. I sit down with each counter manger one by one, and we go over what they will present. They have a total of ten minutes to speak about what they are going to do for a bonus. I put them into teams. For example, my

Palm Desert manager may team up with my Riverside counter manager. Teaming up also reminds them that we are a family and are here to support one another; when they need help, they can look back at their notes and call on a team partner for support. These meetings have excited the counter managers and their teams. The teams have come up with great ideas and events such as having an Oscar party, complete with the red carpet, the team dressing in ball gowns, and buying little Oscar statues to put on the table. A lot of other cosmetic lines have bonuses as well, but my team puts on amazing events, and we have had great increases because of them. We follow the process of approach, consultation, and service linking to a product.

Training a Beauty Advisor on Makeup
When training a beauty advisor, I find out what his or her strong points are. For example, everyone is focused on something in particular when it comes to makeup, whether it's lips, eyes, foundation, or blush. The beauty advisor needs to focus on that area. If it's her lips, we start there. I show her that there are many lip colors: rich, matte, and sheer. Let's not forget the colors in a family, such as roses, reds, and beiges. I teach the beauty advisor to apply a little foundation with a lip brush to neutralize the lip. Then I have her blot with a tissue. I apply a neutral lip pencil to the advisor's lips. We want to use a color that matches the shade of the advisor's or customer's lips. We can also use rose or red. I show her how to stay within the line, going around the entire mouth. Use short connecting strokes, staying within the lip line. Apply lipstick in the middle of the lip, working outward and staying within the lip. Add lip gloss only in the center of the lip. That will give the perfect baby-doll look. I have that beauty advisor repeat the look on me, and her homework is to perfect her customer's lip look.

In our next training, we focus on eyes. I train the beauty advisor to make sure that eye shadow color agrees with the customer's complexion. I make sure that she puts a little foundation or concealer on the eyelids. We want to apply colors like brown, beige, or mauve to the lid, using a little in the crease of the eye and taking it to the lower lash line. Applying color creates more drama. I explain that for a clean look, she should blend really well. To add brightness, add a little shimmer or a bone color.

For a smoky look, line the eye completely with eyeliner and add eye shadow in a round shape, adding more eye shadow up to the crease of the eye. A lot of people think that the colors always have to be black, grey, or brown. That's not true; you can explore many different colors—don't be afraid to try. For an oval, eye shadow should be on the lid and lash line. Apply more shadow to the crease of the eye. For a horizontal eye, use a brush, creating angles up and out from the outer eye. That creates a wonderful lifting effect for the eye.

When training the beauty advisor on cheek color, I teach her that applying blush to a brush from the back of her hand will regulate the intensity. Have the customer smile, and then apply the flat part of the brush to the skin in a circular motion with a sweep toward the hairline. Training the advisor on foundation is key. I show her that three swipes on the center of the face in cool, neutral, and warm undertones will help the customer in choosing her foundation. I also suggest that the customer take a mirror and go outside in the sunlight, because sometimes one can't see the color in the store because the lighting is dull.

When training my advisors to do eyebrows, I teach them to comb the eyebrow to the arch, making sure it's about two-thirds of the distance from the brow. Draw a line from arch to outer eyebrow, find the angle she wants to create, and draw toward the arch of the eyebrow using light and dark shades.

When training my beauty advisor on eyeliner, I teach them to hold the pencil or brush in a slanted position in the middle of the lid, and to have the beauty advisor or customer tilt her head. Start from the inner corner of the eye and don't pause.

When training the beauty advisor on applying mascara, I tell her to apply it to the base of the lashes with lifting motions. After applying mascara, comb with a mascara brush to separate lashes. If you are using an eyelash curler, make sure you curl the lash before you apply mascara. Make sure you have good, clean makeup brushes to support your look!

I notice after the beauty advisor is trained, her confidence level improves, and she is able to instill confidence in her customers. When the customers are satisfied, they become loyal to the beauty advisor. The beauty advisor now becomes the master of the brush and can start teaching the customer the techniques for applying makeup and taking care of her skin.

Image is so important as a beauty advisor. Your image can make or break you, so dress to impress! I believe it always starts with the leader, and that means it starts with me. I always make sure that my hair is neat, my makeup is done, and my clothes are pressed. My nails and toenails are done, and my shoes are not turned over. When I train my beauty advisors, I let them know that they should never come to work looking like they just got out of bed. I remind them that they are in the beauty world, and they should look better than everyone in the store.

I know what you are thinking: "Is that really achievable in a real world?" The answer is yes. Why not take some time to pamper yourself every day? Most women and men don't take the time. I explain to my beauty advisors that that's why customers come to them. They must take the time as beauty advisors to pamper themselves every day before they come into work. Not only will they have a wonderful attitude, but they will attract customers.

Their chairs should never be empty! Booking customers during the week can be a challenge. I train my beauty advisor to book the customer during the week that you are training to do makeup and training on how to take care of skin. Have a makeup or skin workshop. I came up with the name "the workshop bar" because we put the stools at the counter and have about four at a time for each session. That really helps the beauty advisor: instead of asking the customers to come get their makeup done, the beauty advisor is asking to let her teach how to put on makeup. The beauty advisor stands behind the counter and leads the session, starting with primer, foundation, concealer, and loose powder. The makeup session is about an hour and goes on throughout the day. If it is skincare, the session is run the same way, with a focus on skincare. I explain that they should save the weekends for events, and usually it is very successful.

Being a good leader has nothing to do with age. Take for example, my husband, who joined the Marines at twenty years old and had to jump into fifteen feet of water. There was just one problem: he couldn't swim! My husband was able to get through it, but the leadership came from my son years later, when he was ten years old and taught my husband how to swim. He was able to teach my husband basic skills at ten years old with patience and a lot of fun!

In a leadership role, patience is key. I also believe in blessing the people who work for you. Something as simple as buying lunch or buying a coffee card for your beauty advisors and your makeup artists shows that you appreciate them. "Give and it should be Given to you" (Luke 6:38). Being a blessing becomes so much easier when you don't expect anything back.

Don't judge a book by its cover! I remember when I was behind the counter as a beauty advisor, and there was this one lady who came in who was not dressed the best. She had stringy hair and would go from counter to counter asking for samples to put into her bag. The girls began to call her the bag lady. I was able to introduce myself to her one day and show her some of my products. I'm not going to lie: I thought in my mind she was a bag lady too. After speaking to her, I found out she was pretty well off, and she ended spending two hundred dollars with me. Even years later, when I'm in a store, I see her pass through. Even though I'm with a different retailer, she still takes the time to say hello.

The lesson is to never judge a book by its cover; instead, get to know the person, even if she is going from counter to counter. Introduce yourself and ask if she needs help. Take a product in your hand from your line and do a demo. Ask if she would like a facial or a makeover. Find something about her to compliment. Treating people right should always be the focus. "(Do not judge by appearances, but judge with right judgment" (John 7:24).

Health and healing taking care of your temple is key. Eat the right foods! I have always been a healthy eater but since I had been dealing with proteinura, I really have to watch what I'm eating: no salt, very limited meat, and very limited protein. It has taken some time to get used to, but I'm starting to feel better. I have decided I have no choice and am going to keep fighting by using my faith. It seems like I was going through a mourning period, almost if I was giving up. I said *almost*, but my faith would not allow me to give up. "So that your faith might not rest in the wisdom of men but in the power of God" (1 Cor. 2:5). I had chemotherapy to treat my body. I thought, I'm in the beauty industry, so how can I show my face? I will lose my hair. What can I do? First I prayed. I realized if I had to get some hair sewed in, it was still mine because I'd bought it. For a year, I had been dealing with broken blood vessels in the eye. One minute I was a size four, and the next thing I knew, I was a thirteen or fourteen. I felt like I was in a scene from *The Nutty Professor* with Eddie Murphy, when he was changing in size. It was a lot for one person to go through, and I know that there are people that are going through worse.

At the time you are going through any kind of sickness or disease, you are thinking about how you are going to get through it. I know that sounds selfish, but I'm being real. I even thought about my mother, who was in the World Trade Center. She ran down eighty-eight flight of stairs. As she and her friend got to the bottom of the stairs, my mother's friend decided to go one way, and my mother went the other. They hugged, and as the building was falling, my mother ran and collapsed. She woke up in the hospital. Little did she know she would get lung cancer from that years later. My mother has battled a lot in life, from having to raise three girls on her own to helping raising grandchildren. Who am I to complain?

As I started to be a blessing to people, and I started to pray for people, it took the focus off of me. As Dr. Robert L. Wilks says, God is taking you somewhere! There's an ease that you are walking in! That includes my beauty advisors. I'm not a doctor, but it is important that my advisors take care of themselves. They can't help their teams if they are not at their best. Part of that is eating a healthy diet and drinking a lot of water.

Leading is not just giving orders. As a leader, you should never go in, point a finger, and say, "Do this and do that." Being a good leader means you roll up your sleeve and work with your beauty advisor for example stock. Create a list with all products and go through the drawers together to see what's needed for the counter. Show her as the products get low, she can log them so we can send in more beforehand, and they can have products to sell.

I had a trainer whom I respected as a leader, and I will tell you why. I was with my team in the store, and we were very busy; everyone had someone in her chair or was ringing up a customer. The trainer was passing through, and it was not her attention to stay. She saw we needed help and didn't ask any questions—she simply rolled up her sleeves and starting doing a facial massage, and she followed up with makeup. The trainer ended up staying for the rest of the day.

You might say, "Isn't that what should be done?" Well, if that was the case, more trainers and executives would do it. There's that old saying that it takes a village. I don't believe one person should ever walk in and pick things apart, especially when you have a beauty advisor who pours her heart and soul into her counter. Even when you have a beauty advisor who is not doing a great job, instead of picking her apart, find away to see If you can work with her. If you can't, at least you have tried all you can to work with that advisor.

Being a mother is one of greatest accomplishments and is the hardest job one will ever have. I often wonder how I have helped other young men and women. I remember I needed a creative way to teach my daughter to wear makeup, so I had a glamour shot party for her sweet sixteen. I had a few of her friends and their mothers attend, and I taught them how to do their makeup. The glamour shot team did their hair and took a glamour shot. They had a wonderful time, and even the mothers took part in the makeup lesson.

Sometimes I wonder if I have done enough for my own children, but then I remember that the Bible says: "Train a child, for when they are old they will not depart." I know that my husband and I have to believe we have raised both of our children right, instilling good values and ethics. Although they have their own ideas, I have to release control and watch the moral values come through. I have to say it is exciting to see it all come to pass; I see my son and daughter say that their dad and I are in their heads. That's a good feeling! We have done our jobs, and now we're there to listen and guide them. I never thought there was so much in being a leader, and you can put this into action in your home and in your business!

Put up or Shut Up!

Being a role model means doing what you say you are going to do. Mean what you say! If you set a date to take your team out for lunch, then do it. If you tell them you are going to be there a certain day to train them, be there. This applies with friends and family as well. How can you ever become a leader if your word doesn't mean anything? Be on time. Being late for anything shows poor leadership. I'm not saying things don't happen, but it should not be a habit. Remember that everything you do is being looked at, even when you think no one is watching!

My husband says that you know you can't be a leader without someone in your life who shows you leadership. My husband is a great example of one who puts God's foundation first. I can honestly say that he is a great example. He is not judgmental. He listens and often says there are two sides to a story, so we should hear both sides. He reminds me of my father in that way, because as a daddy's girl it was always my side, and my father would say, "What about the other person's side? Michelle, there are always two sides to a story!" I had to learn that, and part of that comes from releasing control and releasing pride, thinking of the other person instead of thinking about my needs.

Do you think makeup can cover a hurt spirit? I ask that to Dr. Darlene, who wrote the book *Freedom Positioning System.* This is her reply.

> No, makeup cannot cover up a hurt spirit. If your spirit is hurt, this is something that is seen through your soul; your soul is displayed through your eyes. Makeup can attempt to cover up the foundation of hurt, but it will take a deep cleansing of the spirit to completely heal the spirit. Makeup, just like any other foundation, can cover up the appearance of hurt. Makeup can and will provide a means for a hurt person to function in their dysfunction, but it won't cover up hurt.

For more info on Dr. Darlene's book, go to www.drdarlenewilliams.com.

Monkey See, Monkey Do!

I asked Anita Alexander to think back and remember when she first started to wear makeup. What was her reason for wearing makeup, and how old was she? Anita informed me that she started wearing makeup in junior high school; her reason for wearing makeup was to fit in with the cool girls. As a result, she said her makeup was worn really heavy, and she didn't understand how to put on makeup.

Anita is my sister, and we came from a strict home. My mother did not allow us to wear makeup until we were sixteen, and my mother worked all the time, so I took care of Anita. Instead of me helping her through that process, I was as strict as my mother. Who knew she was wearing her makeup during the day at school and washing it off before she came home?

What this has taught me as a mother is to start teaching my daughter early, and to have teen workshops to get teens involved, as well as the mothers. They should understand that wearing makeup the right way can enhance their beauty while still looking natural.

Pick and Choose Your Battles!

In a leadership role, we should always pick and choose our battles. We sometimes get so overwhelmed that if we are not careful, we can overwhelm our team as well. It's not about who is right or wrong, but finding a middle ground that can help the beauty advisor and her team.

There was a mother and daughter who came in. The daughter was very young, around thirteen, and was in private school. She was very picky: even at such a young age, no matter what cosmetic line she went to, she was not satisfied. Her mother was just as picky.

When they came to my counter, I spoke with my heart and asked the teen what colors she liked. I had her pick out some colors to play with, and then we had fun by teaching her how to put on her own makeup. We were able to laugh and have a good time. I did the same with her mother for skincare and makeup. Years later, that beautiful teen became a beauty advisor and worked for me for a while. I cannot tell you how rewarding it is to watch a customer grow up right in front of your eyes and love the brand so much that she works for it.

Thanks to great leadership from her parents, my niece, who is three years old, waves her hand in the air and says she is a princess. That is great leadership because as Eleena grows up, she will realize that her self-worth is important, and wearing makeup does not make her who she is but will enhance who she is. Often we relate to beauty advisors as bartenders: customers relay what they are going through, and we are there to listen. But we want to make sure that the customers aren't using makeup to cover real issues that they are going through. Being a great leader starts with hearing, sharing, and giving. As Dr. Robert L. Wilks says, "In leadership there are times God will test you, You shouldn't be in Leadership and don't expect to be tested!"

Customer Sharing

Sharon Dash says, "Do you see my hurt spirit? No, because of my makeup. Sometimes if the makeup is a beautiful mask, it can cover my hurt spirit. The beautiful mask can sometimes cover the real me—my heart, my spirit, the mask. The makeup can get me through the day so I can do my job, so I will be there for others until I come home and use a cleanser to take off my makeup, my beautiful mask."

Sharon Dash's sixteen-year-old daughter Jasmine says, "Makeup can't cover a hurt spirit because makeup can only make you a different person on the outside. I try to tell my friends that too much makeup doesn't make you beautiful—they are already beautiful."

Rochelle Jean-Pierre says, "I can't go anywhere without my eyebrows done and my lipstick on. I feel that for me, it brightens my face and enhances my beauty!"

Health

How do you work in the beauty industry with broken eye vessels? I felt like an ugly duckling at this point, knowing that I needed to be there for my team. I had one blood vessel clear up only to have another one pop. This had to stop! I was at a 10.5 instead of a 12.0 for red blood cells, and I was at a 58 percent instead of 90 percent with my kidney due to all the medicine I was taken. I wanted to go in store as a leader, not a hero, meaning that I had something to prove. I didn't want to just continue to teach my beauty advisors and be there for them. "If God is for us, who can be against us?" (Rom. 8:31) I'm still going to work with a smile on my face!

Winning teams
- trust each other;
- respect each other;
- understand each other; and
- enjoy each other.

To give anything less than your best is to sacrifice the gift.
—Steve Prefontaine

Everyone can rise above their circumstances and achieve success if they are dedicated to and passionate about what they do.
—Author

Some people don't leave the house without doing their hair. I don't leave the house without my lipstick. Putting on lipstick is like drawing on a smile to help you face the day!
—Dawana Gary

Behind the Lipstick
Natasha Jean-Pierre

Behind these doors,
Behind these four walls,
Behind the lipstick, I cry
An inner cry that has broken all damns.

Damn, I'm tired of crying.
So I reach down in my designer bag and pull out a stick of Juicy Fruit.
Now I'm chewin' hard as hell,
Still crying.
It's so hard to stop once I've started.
It's so hard to remember how it all began.
But when I remember, I'll tell myself again,
Because I am my own best friend.

Please stop,
I tell myself—
A weak attempt to gain control.
Everything is going to be all right.
I offer myself some comfort.

When what I really want is a shot of Southern Comfort,
A stick of gum is not enough to convince the world
That I can handle this thing called life.

I chase this man around,
His shadow,
Looking for the right time to ease my hand in his.
I wait on his arrival
Like black folk wait on another leader for survival.

Ruby red, passion fruit,
My illusion, my lipstick, my façade—
I wear it as thick as a lie.
Behind my lipstick is where I hide,
Pretending to be happy,
Never really knowing what that means.
But I know what it looks like,
And today it's ruby red.

Reach one, teach one. It was so good to get back to work and see my beauty advisors. I had been gone for four months, and there were a lot of tears and hugs. I woke up, my eye was clear, and I had great energy. I felt so good and was smiling in the mirror as I looked at myself a new state of mine a new outlook. Being even more of a blessing to my team.

I'm finding out that I have some new teams in some of my stores. There are new beauty advisors to train, so as I go step by step with training new beauty advisors, I will make note.

It was so good to spend the day with my team. One of my beauty consultants had a chance to train me! That felt so good. She trained me in strobing, a method that you can use to highlight your face. She did a wonderful job. I can't tell you how proud I was of her to see her take control and learn her craft.

When working with your beauty advisor, you want to make sure that she can teach you something. Have her be the trainer for the day! That will give her the confidence to be able to speak to the customer and understand the product.

I had an interesting day with my new trainer. She came up with her new way of training beauty advisors by using a system she developed called DEFEATS.

>Demo (facial service)
>Example (through relationship)
>Features (benefits)
>Experience (testimony)
>Analogy
>Tools, such as iPod for consultation
>Statistics

The evidence of DEFEATS is improving the beauty advisor's selling skills and teaching her that she will be able to think out of the box by finding out what the strength of the product is. She can break it down so that the customer can understand without making it too technical.

She explained to me it's not about right or wrong when talking about the product; it's all in the delivery. For example, when she was training me on the new products, she asked me to sell it back to her. Right away I said, "Hey. wait a minute. I'm just back from medical leave! I haven't been to school, and I don't even have the product book!"

She said, "Michelle it's not about being out sick or being right or wrong. Just from me telling you a little about the product, sell it to me."

I put DEFEAT into motion. It worked, and I was very excited. That is a training tool that I will use with my beauty advisors.

Today I put DEFEAT into motion while still training without a workbook! I worked with a new beauty advisor, and she did great. I was able to explain to her the DEFEAT concept. She understood and has now put it into action. I will be training all the beauty advisors on this concept. One of my other beauty advisors also put DEFEAT into motion, and she had one sale for over five hundred dollars! It is a great concept, and she ran with it.

You have to deal with so many different personalities in my position, so you have to wear many hats. Each beauty advisor is different. I do believe that if you treat people right and give them respect, they will work with you. Now, don't get me wrong, there are some whom I have encountered who didn't always do that.

How do you handle it when one of your team members is unhappy with the team and the job? The first thing you want to do is have a talk with your beauty advisor to see what is making her unhappy about the team and the job. You want to try to get her excited about the job again. If she has fallen out of love with the job and can't fall back in love, then maybe it's time for her to move on, but at least give her a chance to figure it out can you can correct the problem.

For example, I had two beauty advisors who were top sellers and worked the same shift on the same team. They couldn't get along, and there were always complaints about the other one stealing customers. It got to the point where one was going to leave. I had a one-on-one conversation with each girl and let them vent. I reminded them that the customer belonged to the product, and any beauty advisor on the team could help them. After I made them understand, I brought them in together and explained how we should be able to work as a team, and how we could advance more by helping each other. They hugged, and I had no more problems. They thanked me for taking the time to solve the issue.

A leader should be able to be objective!

> The quality of a person's life is in direct proportion
> to their commitment to excellence regardless
> of their chosen field of endeavor.
> —Vince Lombardi

> Excellence is an art won by training and habituation. We do
> not act rightly because we have virtue or excellence, but
> we rather have those because we have acted rightly.
> —Author

> We are what we repeatedly do. Excellence,
> then, is not an act but a habit.
> —Aristotle

I've added a new concept to training, called three reasons a season. It's about why the customer should come back to see you. The whole point is to build up the customer's loyalty to you and the product. Once you have done that, you are giving that customer the information and proper care to build a relationship and help her take care of her skin and makeup. You can teach the real reason behind wearing makeup and not getting caught up in an industry that revolves around concealment and vanity.

The most dangerous thing we can ever do is get caught into a trend instead of knowing the real us. At the same time, we also want to make sure we don't stay in a time warp. Staying true to ourselves is a key factor, and finding the right beauty advisor and product line will help.

You should make sure you are doing your research on the best product line for you, and getting the right consultation is very important.

Rochelle Quezada was asked, "Do you think makeup can cover a hurt spirit?"

I think a hurt spirit is something that has to be addressed separately without makeup. It is like when you realize you might have to take off a few pounds, but you ignore it until one day you stand in front of a mirror naked, and you say, "Today is the day." Renewing your mind renews your spirit. Changing the way you think on a daily basis is the key to the spirit!

We often hear the phrase "Mind, body, and soul." Proverbs 17:22 states, "A cheerful heart is good medicine, but a crushed spirit dries up the bones."

Where There's a Will, There's a Way

Being a good leader is also coming up with creative ways to encourage your beauty advisors when they lose their motivation. One beauty advisor was frustrated because she felt that she would always have to leave her cosmetic line to go help in fragrance. I suggested to her that she take her appointment book with her, and as she introduced herself to the customers and took care of what they needed, she could invite them to have a service or make an appointment if they couldn't do the service at the time. The beauty advisor was very excited about it and said she would have never thought of that. It is a good way to promote the business, and most of all, you are helping the customers.

It was such an inspiration when one of my beauty advisors told me how much I inspired her. She was promoted to another line as counter manager, and she told me how she had to do a national event on a weekday instead of a weekend—and it was 4.0 goal! She was able to do 5.0 and said she'd used what she'd learned when she worked with me. I was so proud of her. The great thing is that she still works with my team, and she still helps out our line a lot. A lot of managers in the work force get bothered because they say they are stealing secrets. One of the things I learned over the years is to teach one is to reach one!

Training a new beauty advisor requires image standards and guidelines. The focus is a comprehensive understanding of all products, usage, and techniques. When training products, we want to train with using these questions: What it is? What does it do? What will I see? Who is it for? How do I use it?

I want my girls to
- be proficient at all counter demonstrations and service skills;
- master consultations and makeup along with skincare; and
- have consistent and successful follow-up skills.

I was able to work with a new beauty advisor today, and we had a great time on these aspects. At the end of a great day, I watched as she was able to be comfortable and help a customer apply makeup.

Great leaders unleash potential in others.
- Empower: Expand your knowledge.
- Explore: Develop your team to take ownership, putting team members in charge of different responsibilities. For example, create excitement by putting each team member in charge of an event.
- Equip: Always giving your beauty advisor all information and training to sharpen her skills.

Putting on My Big Girl Panties

I woke up feeling good, and the next thing I knew, I popped a blood vessel at lunchtime. What do you do when you know your day isn't over, but you just want to go home, thinking that you aren't beautiful enough to help people and feeling like a frog waiting for your prince to kiss you so you can turn into a princess? What do you do? You put on your big girl panties, hold up your head, and keep moving. I sat a customer down and put on her makeup, and she brought what I put on her, broken vessel and all. As Psalm 30:2 says, "O Lord my God, I called to you for help and you healed me."

It started in April 2014. I had just flown back from a meeting in San Francisco when I noticed the swelling in my face. I felt dizzy and blotted.

I had just had my regular doctor checkup in January, and everything was okay.

I went to the doctor but didn't see my regular one. This new one said I looked okay and sent me home. Meanwhile, my blood pressure was really high, which was unusual for me because I had never had a problem with it before. I saw my regular doctor, and she could not understand it herself, so she ran some test and said she was sending me to a kidney specialist. I saw the kidney doctor, and she said that she wanted me to have a biopsy.

I did, and it came back that I had minimal change disease, which only happened in children. At that point the kidney was linking protein, and the protein was setting off the blood pressure and swelling; it set off the whole body. To treat the protein, she put me on a medication called prodazone, which I came to find out was just a bandage and not a treatment. Within two months of taking that medicine, I was all clear, but the same thing happened again. At that point, after months of going back and forth and seeing a second specialist, I was told that I would need chemo. The first chemo was for eight weeks, and for a month I did well. Then I relapsed. My doctor did a second biopsy, and it still showed minimal change disease, but it also showed a touch of gleomerulosclerois, which was a scarring on the kidney. The objective was to get the protein down to the level it was supposed to be. Now I'm on a different kind of chemo that works with the blood flow of the body. The doctors don't know how this happen This chemo is set for a year, and I believe in God. I believe in my healing, and every day I'm confessing and meditating on what the word of God says.

Isaiah 58:8 states, "Then your light will break forth like the dawn, and your healing will quickly appear: then your righteousness will go before you, and the glory of the Lord will be your rear guard." Now, I want to be real clear! I am not writing about what I'm going through for people to feel sorry for me, because I have strong faith, and I'm doing just fine! I am writing about this because I want to bring awareness about getting your kidneys checked, as well as eating healthy. Speak to your doctor about a great food plan. Changing the way I eat was also a big part of my recovery. I thought I ate pretty healthy, but there were still some things I had to cut out of my diet.

Ambassador Program

Staying connected to your beauty advisor is a must. Having a connection with people you know at work is another thing. That's why the Ambassador Program was developed for all my beauty advisors. They have embraced this program and are very excited. This program has produced great results.

The objective was to connect with two to three friends in the department that would discover and help build their businesses. Here are some tips on building your network of friends.

- Connect with two to three people in your department whom you know well.
- The best time to build your network is before you need something; offer to help first.
- Be genuine to build long-term relationships.
- You don't have to know a lot of people, just the right people.
- Focus on finding people who are relevant to you. As time goes on, you can decide if the interests that you share with someone are worth pursuing further. It's better to have three people willing to help you out than it is to have five hundred who simply know your name.
- Go beyond your department and connect with people in various departments.

Continuing to Build the Relationship
- Use the helpful approach.
- Spread information in a helpful way as you introduce products to your friends; share why you love the product.
- Make networking a habit, and make a appointment to follow up within one week.
- Try to make one connection a day; it's five minutes of your day.
- Follow up with your friends to make sure they don't have questions, and to see how they like the product.

The Magic Number Is Three

Contacting customers throughout the year is so important. Here are the three reasons.

1. Prepare
    - Review your entire customer list.
    - Determine how many customers to contact per day.
2. Contact
    - For each customer, write down three reasons for why you are contacting them.
    - Sample new product.
    - Plan events.
    - Birthdays.
    - Be prepared for services they may require.
3. Follow-up
    - Go through your customer list within two weeks.
    - One weekly call with your reason for the season. By the end of two weeks, you should be able to touch a whole new customer base.

Following these three concepts for customers to return and see the beauty advisor it is a road map to building a foundation to business.

Here's a concealing trick for those who feel they have a rounder face and want their face to look thinner. Take a shade darker concealer. Start from your for head and make the number three going into the cheek as well as the jawline. Take your brush and sweep in a upward position.

The Difference between a Boss and a Leader

Recently I sat down with three of my bosses, and the meeting went well. This is why!

Bosses do the following:
- Drive employees
- Depend on authority
- Inspire fear
- Say "I"
- Place blame for the breakdown

- Know how it is done
- Use people
- Take credit
- Command
- Say, "Go"

Leaders do the following:
- Coach others on goodwill
- Generate enthusiasm
- Say "We"
- Fix the breakdown
- Show how it is done
- Develop people
- Give credit
- Ask
- Say, "Let's go"

> Leadership is the capacity to translate vision into reality.
> —Warren Bennis

Why is there a change in floor plan when we are right in the middle of bonus? I learned to take one day at a time. So what if there is a case move, along with Christmas sets out with a whole new case change? This counter is over a half million and ranks number five in the whole department. Why would they do this to us right now? The team is stressed.

As a good leader, how do I handle this? I begin by motivating the team. A good lunch is a start—food is always good for the soul. We then work together by relieving the girls to be able to make phone calls for their bonus, and we work to help the counter manager as much as possible.

We plan to have a great time for the bonus by getting a DJ, and we decided to have a red carpet event. We have a photo shoot for the customers. The whole team is very excited. My plan is to keep them focus on this big event. The vision is to keep the team on track and have a successful event with everything that is going on, because in reality we have 60.5 to get in a few weeks, and the show must go on!

Before you are a leader, success is all about growing yourself.
When you become a leader, success is all about growing others.
—Jack Welch

He Loves Me!

It's been a year since I went through my bloody eyes issue. What do you do when the protein in your body is 6,000, and the range is supposed to near 1.9? It is the month of October, and my anniversary is on the seventeenth. I have been married for twenty-eight years, and I can say this with an honest smile: my husband loves me! I sometimes feel like the princess and the frog. Guess who the frog is? In my case, it's the king and the frog! If just only one kiss could turn my eye clear....

I thank God that my husband loves me unconditionally. I can honestly say that I have found my soul mate. During this whole process, my husband has rushed me to the hospital six times, as well as going into the hospital two times, staying up most of the night, praying, and not accepting bad news. When I could not fix anything to eat, or I needed sometime he was willing to help.

Now, that is what your spouse is supposed to do! Not all spouses try to be as helpful as they should. I thought it would really upset him when I could not see my way, and I gave my husband and my mother my burial arrangements. He said, "I won't receive this." He was not saying that we should not be prepared, but that he would not accept me giving up! As far as my mother, I think her blood pressure went sky high, but she is okay! After the shock was over, my mother and my husband prayed for me.

"Love is patient, and love is kind. It does not envy, it does not boast, and it is not proud. It is not rude, it is not self-seeking, it is not easily angered, and it keeps no record of wrongs. Love does not delight in evil but rejoices with the truth. It always protects, trusts, hopes, and perseveres." This is what we have based our marriage on for twenty-eight years. Thank you to my husband for being there. I love you!

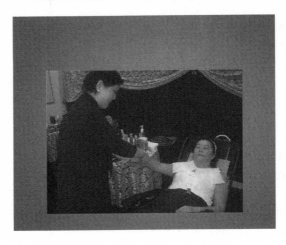

The best executive is the one who has sense enough to pick
good men to do what he wants done, and self- restraint
to keep from meddling with them while they do it.
—Theodore Roosevelt

Training this week has been so exciting. I was able to train two
beauty advisors, and we had so much fun. When I got through training
one of the beauty advisors, I was able to get four new customers. This
beauty advisor has never worked in cosmetics before. Her first day of
training, she did what we call Ayle style, and that is going around the
store and getting new customers. Then on top of that, she was helping
another line and was able to link her own line of product to the sale.

In leadership, I believe in having fun! I like to do a lot of role playing,
as well as go out with the advisor and meet new customers, having
them watch me first and then do it themselves. As we were spreading
the news throughout the departments, I felt proud as that new beauty
advisor took the bull by the horns and brought the new customers to
our counter. Yes, I think she is going to work out just fine!

The leadership instinct you are born with is the backbone. You
develop the funny bone and wish bone that go with it.
—Elaine Agather

One of my beauty advisors was upset that she thought I thought
she was in a bad mood. She needed to vent, and I was there to listen.
She felt bad about her venting, but we all need someone to vent to. I'm
just glad I was there to listen.

A great teacher is not going to tell you! A great
teacher is going to tell you when!
—Dr. Robert L. Wilks

I have had some wonderful trainers over my fifteen years, and I
really treasure them. If I could package each one of them, I would, from
the way they dress to the way they teach. Every trainer is different. I
always embrace what the trainer has to say, because my job is to take it
back to the beauty advisor and the customers. I will always remember

one trainer saying to me, "Listen with your heart, and always have an open spirit to hear what your beauty advisor and customers are saying." This trainer has a special place in my heart because she has always run her business like that, and she always made a plan every year. She told me to be prayed up every day and let the spirit of God flow through me. I believe she was a godsend. I will always be thankful for the time I spent with her.

Are you looking in the mirror and wondering whether your beauty will last? That old expression that beauty is skin deep is interesting. It sounds great, but when you are in the beauty world, you are always in the mirror and looking at skin, makeup, hair, your clothes, and your shoes. You have to wonder, "Am I vain? Or do I have to be aware because it's my job? Should I feel guilty because I like all the above?"

Well, the answer is yes to all! Yes, I look in the mirror to see if my beauty is lasting! Yes, I'm vain!
Yes, I feel guilty because I stay stuck in the mirror and looking at me!

Since I have been going through this illness, I continue to look every couple of minutes. That has to stop because I'm more than just an image in the mirror.
I have so much more to give to my beauty advisors and customers, and to my family. Losing my hair and swelling around the eyes and face is not going to break me! I will be even better. I try to stay out of the mirror for that reason. When I look in the mirror today, it will be because I'm empowering myself to be the best I know I can be.

When you're a leader, you have everyone looking and listening to every word you say and do. Today I had to encounter a beauty advisor who couldn't stop her negative thinking. After going through what I have gone through, I can say I'm in recovery. You start to realize how negatively can affect you. Now, I refuse to take it in. As a leader, how do you handle your beauty advisor when she starts speaking that way? You don't! You refocus her on what she needs to do for the day, and you listen and let her vent some things that are negative but aren't worth responding to. You smile and say, "Let's refocus our day to have the best day possible."

Self-worth is so important, and I teach my beauty advisors to remember that what they think about themselves can affect their businesses. They must take care of themselves first. That's why at the company I work for, we give the beauty advisor a facial and makeup. We want them to understand that without them feeling good about themselves, the customers won't receive the full benefit. We must pamper ourselves daily. Taking the time to be by ourselves is so important, because we get to know who we are, and we need that time to ourselves.

And We Are Off!

This week is our bonus week! It's almost like a race; the teams are pushing to pick up their deficit, and this can put them on top, even for the year. We have events called the Red Carpet to the Bonus Party. The teams are excited and really look forward to this time.

As a leader you want to make sure you are there for your team to support them. A little goes a long way. Something as simple as bringing sandwiches for the team shows them that you care. A coffee card or even a hug makes the team feel empowered. Be there for your team. Show them you care, even if it's something as simple as flowers from your garden or baking a batch of cookies. I remember my trainer baking me a batch of cookies while I was on medical leave. It made me feel so good that she cared to do that, and they tasted great. Use your special talents to help support your teams!

As a leader, remember that the customers come first.

I am learning how to walk away from people and situations that threaten my peace of mind, self-respect, and self-worth!

You must take time for yourself.
- Teams win
- Give back
- Integrity always
- Results matter

Remember, you can't fly with one wing! Love yourself!

I was so sad when a customer, who was a beautiful brown-skinned woman, said she wanted to be white. My mouth dropped because not only did she want to be white, but she wanted a product to start turning her white right there in her chair. As a woman, I just wanted to say, "Love yourself!" As a leader, I want to teach her how to love herself.

My advice was to another beauty advisor to help her be comfortable in her skin by teaching her makeup tips—not to lighten her skin, but to enhance her beauty. We explained to her how beautiful she was with the skin she had, making an appointment with her to show her the latest new makeup and the right way to take care of her skin.

Beauty is not about bleaching your skin or piling on tons of makeup. It is about loving yourself inside and out mind, body and spirit. That is something that has to happen on a daily basis. The makeup industry can have you believing that you must look a certain way, and if you are not careful, you will fall right into it. When the customer left the counter, she was pleased with the results. The beauty consultant was able to get through to this customer and is booking her back for her next makeup workshop. We are not surgeons or doctors. As leaders, we are there to help the customers' spirits as well as their makeup concerns.

Do you think makeup can cover a hurt spirit?
Janay Sanders Shuler

I don't think that makeup can cover a hurt spirit. However, I do believe that it can mask the hurt. Your spirit is something inside of you that can only be changed with internal cleansing. I love makeup and sometimes use it as a tool to make myself feel better. It makes me feel beautiful when I walk outside. I may have had a bad night and woke up with puffy eyes. Due to this, I would use makeup to cover the puffiness of my eyes. Some women are abused by their spouses, and they use makeup cover their scars. Women want to feel and look their best at all times. Makeup doesn't cover a hurt spirit; it gives that hurt spirit something to look forward to.

As a leader, there should be several business standards that you set every day with your beauty advisors.

- Create a unique atmosphere that attracts customers with a warm smile and a comfort zone, exceeding every customer's expectations.
- Every customer is touched at the counter with product.
- Offer and perform unique service to every customer, with an emphasis on consultation and makeup.
- Utilize a client record system with every customer at every visit, focusing on the main purpose of the system: individualized customer care and follow-up.

I recently had lunch with two beauty advisors. We had such a great time talking about not only business but also life. As we were talking about life and sharing our stories about family and my health issues, I noticed a tear run down one of the beauty advisor's face. I asked her why she was crying. She said that she was so grateful to be taken out to lunch. No one had cared enough at her previous job to take her or her co-workers to lunch. I told her that I appreciated everything that she and her team member had done so far this season, and I wanted to do something special for them. What she didn't know was that she was blessing me. I have come to understand that when you do something nice for someone, God is watching, and I know that the Bible says in Jeremiah 31:3, "The Lord appeared to us in the past, saying: I have loved you with an everlasting love; I have drawn you with loving kindness." I believe in showing these girls love and understanding. Needless to say, this team is running a 5.62 increase for the year!

What Makes You Unique Makes You Beautiful!

Recently in one of my stores, as I was doing my regular training around the counter, I felt a gentle tap on my shoulder. It was this older gentlemen in his eighties. He told me with a gentle voice that I was beautiful. He said, "They just don't make them like you anymore," and he asked how tall I was. I thanked him and told him I was five feet eleven inches. He then hugged me. That really made my day. I needed to hear that, especially with everything that I had been going through.

Your genes are what make you unique and beautiful not the makeup or even the clothes you wear. It's the God in you! Letting God inside you will have you smiling inside and out, even on days you don't feel like smiling.

Disarm the Alarm!

One of the main tasks as a leader is to disarm the alarm. I had a customer who was upset because she had been into the store a couple of times to get her product. The product was going out of stock, and that was why it had not been in the store. Because the beauty advisor was on leave, no one looked it up in the system to let her know. The first thing we did was find another type of makeup that she could wear. Once we did that, she was satisfied with the product we'd found for her.

When a customer comes in upset, you want to take the time to assure her that you will do the best you can to help her. If you want to keep her on your product line, you have to make sure you keep her happy. Offer to show her another alternative. Offer the client a service and let her know you care. Even though the customer was not happy that the product she loved was being discontinued, she was satisfied with the customer service, because it wasn't just the customer service—it was like taking care of someone in one's family.

After speaking to my mentor, she reminded me about what to do to get the increase I was looking for. She told me to stay in the bigger doors; they would help me pick up the clients I needed. She also reminded me that this was the time to work client by client, and she reminded me to train the beauty advisors to solve a problem with a suggestion. For example, if a customer had droopy eyelids, what could we suggest to lift the eyelids? It is crucial to stay focused on the problem and give a suggestion. Why? Because we are almost at the end of the season!

Although I was out on a medical leave for half of the season, I ended up at 91.3 percent for the spring season. That is credited with my faith and training the beauty advisors. They are a blessing. Now that we are at the end of our season, with twelve weeks left, I want to be at 100 percent to plan.

Prayer Changes Things!

As I sat in my car throwing up on the side of the road from the medicine that I have been taking, I still prayed and believed God. The doctor did not have the last word—my God did, and my faith was strong. As my anointed hairdresser was taking the weave out of my hair, and I saw that my hair was not what it used to be, I remembered my faith and the fact that prayer changes things.

Prayer is what is getting me through! Today I'm feeling more and more like myself. Prayer changes things!

- Life is like a camera.
- Focus on what's important.
- Capture the good times.
- Develop from the negatives.
- If things don't work out, take another shot!

I work with my beauty advisors to take another shot if something isn't going right. We now have nine weeks left in the season, and vendors are trembling because of the numbers. We try to take things in with a grain of salt, but sometimes it becomes a little bit too much when they start asking questions to which they already know the answers. They also start calling the store to see what time you left. It is all human nature, and it's a shame because the coordinators have an investment as well as the vendors. All in all, we have a job to do, and it has to be done.

God has given me an anointed hair dresser. I have to thank God for her! She has kept my hair up, and it has not fallen out any more than it had. I believe through the end of what I'm going through, my hair will return to its regular length, and it will get thicker. Not only is she a hairdresser, but she is a minster as well.

If God Is for You, Who Can Be Against You?

When you have other executives who try to set you up because they feel you are no longer beneficial, you must stay calm. Document every conversation and save every e-mail. Continue to work with your team by giving them the best direction you can. I promise you when you do not react, things will settle down. As for me, I go into prayer and continue to do the best job I can.

There is this old saying that when you try to kill a king, you'd better not miss. I believe everybody has to answer to somebody. They need to remember to treat people right. When you start mistreating people and place blame so you as an executive don't get in trouble, that's wrong. I have seen it happen so many times over the years.

This industry is very small, and I learned that you never know who you are going to run into: people with whom you use to work, or people who may have been your peers but now were your bosses. You never know. The pitfalls of this industry are real. There have been certain things said, like "It's either you or me!" or "If you feel that, you can't handle the job!" You should not say these things as a boss. A boss should be inspiring, not stressful!

> *Do you think makeup can cover a hurt spirit?*
> Ashley Bond

> My eyebrows and hair are everything!
> Makeup does not define you!
> Staying groomed with good brows and beautiful locks
> are everything!
> When people see you natural with just a touch of
> makeup, I feel you are not covering up—you are
> enhancing what you already have!

> Go confidently in the direction of your dreams!
> Live the life you've imagined.
> —Henry David Thoreau

You know, this year has been so interesting! I heard a pastor say, "Instead of wondering why, just say what. What can I do to resolve the problem? What can I do to help? What can I do not to sound harshly when speaking to upper management? What can we do to help people in need?"

When you ask yourself these questions, you often take your mine off yourself and focus on helping someone else. In this industry, we must learn that everyone has a different way of learning, and although we are so passionate about our jobs, we must not forget that people have feelings. I'm not saying we have to walk on eggshells, but we must listen more with our hearts to understand how we can help a person. It doesn't matter whether or not you are training a person or listening to a friend.

We are approaching 2016, and I'm excited about the new year. I look forward to all my stores making plan. I think with clear communication and the new strategy that my team came up with, we will make plan. Our strategy is that we have the main focuses of the season. The training team, other executives, and I meet and then put together the focus on a sheet that the beauty consultants can follow throughout the season. On the sheet is a phone script along with explaining the product, as well as an event sheet so the team can plan an event around the product focus. It helps the team focus on the new products for the season. The team likes this new concept. The account coordinators and the trainers like this focus as well because it is easy to train, and it is also is to follow up.

> *Do you think makeup can cover a hurt sprit?*
> Mary L. McCall

> Makeup cannot cover a hurt spirit. Trusting in the Lord is the only way your spirit will heal. As for myself, makeup makes me feel young and refreshed. Makeup makes me look like years flew by. Makeup makes me feel like a Georgia peach hanging on a tree and waiting to be plucked!

Good Relationships

Just recently I had an experience I will never forget. I was in one of my stores when I received some packages I had recently purchased. One of the beauty consultants said that loss prevention did not want purchases on the floor. I told the beauty consultant that I did not have my car and was waiting for my husband to pick up the purchases. I said not to worry about it; loss prevention could come speak to me.

The next thing I knew, that beauty consultant took a break, and loss prevention came over and told me to take my bags upstairs. I explained my situation, and she still had an attitude and demanded I take them upstairs. I was on the phone with another executive, and I told her when I finished, I would take them upstairs. Before I could do that, her boss came down and said because I had an attitude with his detective, I had to leave the store. He warned that he did not want to embarrass me by calling mall security.

I told him, "Let's go upstairs." I went to the store manager, with whom I had a great relationship, and explained what happened. The man continued to have an attitude, and I explained to him that I was here to help the store, and he should not speak to anyone like he and his detective had spoken to me. The store manager apologized to me and assured me that it was okay.

Instead of blaming the beauty consultant for calling loss prevention, which I didn't have proof of, I loved her even more and did not discuss with anyone what happened upstairs. A good manager moves on and focuses on what she came to do!

> *Do you think makeup can cover a hurt spirit?*
> Cristeen Millar
>
> Makeup is a temporary fix in an attempt to improve or enhance one's self-image. Makeup can possibly affect a hurting emotion, but it is a superficial bandage. Makeup may enable people to feel better about themselves on the outside, enough to provoke steps to necessary change. The difference between hurt spirit and a wounded emotion is that the core essence of our spirit is the Lord. We must seek salvation and a personal relationship with him on a daily basis, walking our Christian life and keeping Christ as the center focus.

That is what truly works on a hurt spirit, to allow the Lord to heal us!

In order for our hurt spirits to be healed, we must be willing to make the changes the Lord is asking of us, in order to keep our sinful nature submitted in obedience to God's word!

The bottom line: makeup may affect our hurt emotions, but not our hurt spirits. They are two different things.

Do you think makeup can cover a hurt spirit?
Gary Bond

According to Peter 3:3, Whose adorning of plaiting the hair, and of wearing gold, or of putting on apparel, But let it be the hidden man of the heart, in which is not corruptible, even the ornament of a meek and quiet spirit, which is in the sight of God of great price." Keep the makeup on the outside and the Holy Spirit on the inside.

I will end this way. When I was younger, I had makeup on in all of these situations.

- Jumping over the church pew to beat up a girl who rolled her eyes at me during church service.
- Hitting an ex-boyfriend over the head with a frying pan.
- Slapping my nail lady because she didn't do my nails right.

The only reason I'm telling you these things is because it wasn't the makeup that healed the hurting spirit, which in my case was anger from many things. It was the Lord who healed me and made me the woman who stands before you now. Makeup and the clothes I wore only showed the outside of what people thought I stood for, but once they got to know that person, they did not like her very much!

My grandmother use to say, "Suge, I want you to know that treating people right is so important." My grandmother loved people so much that she had people fighting over which bedroom they were going to stay in, and she only had two bedroom! It was called Southern hospitably, and she made sure she had the best sheets and the greatest food. She loved God and used to say, "Love one another as you love yourselves."

As I got older and started in the cosmetic industry, it dawned on me that it was not an accident that I was here. I started to do facials, which was required by the company I worked for, but I went a step beyond and started massaging feet as well. The next thing I knew, by using all the necessary tools provided by the company, I ended up taking that counter to 250. Within two years I became an account coordinator. I have been an account coordinator for fifteen years. I had an excellent trainer who raised me in the product knowledge and tradition of the company. I will never forget her passion and her being called the mother of our region. This trainer is a legend because those of us who call ourselves her children still carry on what she has taught us.

Remember that proud people want their dreams to come true. They are always concerned about what people think. People with humility only concern themselves with what God thinks about them. If you think the way God thinks, all your dreams will come true!

My *Divine Foundation* is simply this: "Remember as a person thinks so are they" (Prov. 23:7). I use all the proper tools given to me and listen with my heart rather than judge anyone, and this has helped my career. Teaching beauty consultants to be the best they can be and to love people is the key, even before teaching products and everything involving makeup. You can't help anyone else if you don't help yourself first.

Remember to always take time for yourself! For me, it starts with prayer. Then I begin to pamper myself as I start my day. Don't get caught up in a world of pitfalls in the industry. Instead, get caught up in loving people and letting them see the beautiful spirit that is in you!

Hairdresser: Mikell Bellamy Sanders
Makeup: Shiseido Cosmetics
Suit: BEBE

Unity is strength ... when there is teamwork and
collaboration, wonderful things can be achieved.
—Mattie J.T Stepanek

If your actions inspire others to dream more, learn more,
do more and become more, you are a leader.
—John Quincy Adams

Leaders don't create followers, they create more leaders.
—Tom Peters

A good leader listens and talks to the team to find the
individual strengths of each team member.
—Author

A team is a group of people contributing to achieve a common goal.
—Author

A leader's attitude is caught by his or her followers
more quickly than his or her actions.
—John C. Maxwell

A good leader is a person who takes a little more than his
share of the blame and little less than his share of credit.
—John C. Maxwell

Acknowledgments

I would like to acknowledge my mother, Mary McCall, and the late Roosevelt McCall for a positive upbringing. My mother worked continually to help her family, and her support is endless. Thank you, Mommy!

A special thank-you to my late grandmother, Molly Dock, who always listened with her heart. Love you, Suge.

I want to thank my sisters, Rochelle and Anita, for always making me laugh even when I didn't feel like laughing. A special thank-you to my brother-in-law D Wayne for encouraging me to write this book. I love you guys!

To all of my nieces and nephews: how I love you dearly, and I thank you for letting me be a part of your lives!

Thanks to my aunts and uncles, and to all my cousins. A special thank-you to Dr. Darlene Williams for encouraging me to write this book.

A special thank-you to my Shiseido family and friends.

Thanks to my pastor, Dr. Robert L. Wilks, for his dedication and teachings.

A special thank-you to First Lady Freda Wilks for speaking into my life!

I want to thank my amazing family! My husband, Gary, and my children, Gary Jr. and Ashley. Thank you for loving me unconditionally. I love you! A family that prays together stays together, and that shows true leadership and is the key to a divine foundation!

A special dedication to my grandmother for instilling my Christian values and the belief that when God says do it, you do it!

41

About The Author

Michelle Bond has worked in the beauty industry for 15 years. At a young age, Michelle had a knack for fashion, modeling, and styling. Her earned success in the beauty industry has provided her a platform to motivate and inspire others. She is dedicated to the positive growth of her teams and encourages them to develop healthy strategies to expand their business. In both personal and professional life, Michelle chooses to focus on helping others while keeping God as her foundation. Michelle currently works in the beauty industry as an Executive Account Coordinator in California.

Made in the USA
Las Vegas, NV
05 March 2022